RUTH
A young woman loses everything and then finds love

and

Esther
A beautiful young orphan becomes the Queen of Persia

Written and Illustrated
by
Pauline Shone

Olive Shoots
Imprint of
OlivePress
צהר זית
Publisher

RUTH
A young woman loses everything and then finds love

and

Esther
A beautiful young orphan becomes the Queen of Persia

Ruth and Esther

"Feed My Sheep" Series

Written and Illustrated by Pauline Shone

Copyright © 2006, 2025 by Pauline Shone, Simon Books, Derbyshire, England, formerly published as two separate books.

ISPN: 978-0-9554445-9-3

All rights reserved. No part of this book may be reproduced or transmitted in any form or by any means—electronic, mechanical, photocopying, or any information stored in a retrievable system,—without the prior permission of the copyright holder, according to USA and UK copyright laws.

Published by
Olive Shoots
an Imprint of:
Olive Press Publisher
www.olivepresspublisher.com
olivepressbooks@gmail.com

All Scripture quotes are taken from the *Holy Bible, New Living Translation*, copyright © 1996, 2004, 2015 by Tyndale House Foundation. Used by permission of Tyndale House Publishers, Inc., Carol Stream, Illinois 60188. All rights reserved.

All pronouns referring to the Trinity are capitalized.

Table of Contents

Ruth 9

FOREWORD	11
Naomi Returns to Bethlehem	12
Ruth Chooses to Stay with Naomi	14
The Journey	16
Barley Harvest	20
Boaz Meets Ruth	22
Boaz's Goodness to Ruth and Naomi	24
Naomi Advises Ruth	25
Ruth Obeys Her Mother-in-Law	27
Boaz Wants To Marry Ruth	28
Boaz Buys Naomi's Land	30
Boaz Marries Ruth	32
Life Is Pleasant	34
Boaz was the father of Obed	37
Obed was the father of Jesse	37
Jesse was the father of King David	37

Ruth Study Notes and Questions 38
God cares about you. 41

Esther 45

FOREWORD	47
Celebrations at the Royal Palace	48
Queen Vashti Insults the King	57
The Search for a New Queen	59
Esther Is Chosen	62
Mordechai Saves The King's Life	64
Haman Plots Against The Jews	66
Haman's Plot to Kill the Jews	68
Panic Among the Jews	69
Mordecai Warns Esther	71
Queen Esther Risks Her Life	73
Haman's Plan to Kill Mordecai	80
Mordecai Is Rewarded	84
The King Executes Haman	88
Mordecai is Honoured	92
Haman's Plot is Defeated	92
The Feast of Purim	96
PRAYER	97
Esther Study Notes and Questions	98
Prayer	107
Thanking God	108
Prayer and Fasting	109
PURIM	110
About the Author	114

RUTH

A young woman loses everything and then finds love

FOREWORD

When Joshua ruled over God's people, they conquered the land of Canaan and named it Israel. But after Joshua's death, the people turned away from God. Then because of their rebellion against God and His laws, Israel was defeated by their enemies, time and time again.

And in those days, a severe famine came upon the land of Israel. So Elimelech left his home in Bethlehem and took his family to the land of Moab. Now when Elimelech died in Moab, his wife Naomi was left alone there with her two sons. And these sons married Moabite women named Orpah and Ruth.

Then about ten years later, Naomi's sons also died. Naomi, heartbroken, believed that God was against her. Well, this is how she felt, but it wasn't true. The God of Israel loved Naomi and He had very special plans for her future. These plans also included her daughter-in-law, Ruth—wonderful plans that would surprise and delight them both!

Ruth

Naomi Returns to Bethlehem

Naomi was all alone in a foreign land, and she often thought of her home in Bethlehem. So when she heard that God was blessing Judah with good crops again, she decided to return.

Naomi and her two daughters-in-law set off on the journey to Bethlehem in Judah. But after the three women had travelled together a little way, Naomi told her daughters-in-law to return to their mothers' homes. She said she hoped that God would reward them for their kindness to her sons and herself. And she prayed that God would bless them with a husband and a home. Then she kissed them both goodbye, and they all began to weep.

Now Orpah and Ruth loved Naomi and did not want to leave. But Naomi asked why they should want to go with her? She was too old to have a husband and bear more sons! But even if it were possible, would they wait for them to grow up? No, it was better for them to return to their parents' home!

Ruth Chooses to Stay with Naomi

Naomi said that the loss of her husband and sons had made her very sad. It seemed that God was against her, and she was deeply sorry that her daughters-in-law had lost their husbands. The three women wept together again. Then Orpah kissed Naomi goodbye, and returned to her people and her gods. But Ruth still clung to her mother-in-law. So Naomi urged Ruth to follow her sister-in-law.

But Ruth replied, "Don't ask me to leave you and turn back. Wherever you go, I will go; wherever you live, I will live. Your people will be my people, and your God will be my God. Wherever you die, I will die, and there I will be buried. May the LORD punish me severely if I allow anything but death to separate us!" Ruth:1:16-18

When Naomi saw that Ruth had made up her mind, she stopped trying to persuade her to leave. So the two women continued together on the journey to Bethlehem in Judah.

The Journey

As the two women travelled, Naomi told Ruth many stories about her home in Bethlehem and the farming life there. There was the wet season, then the time for the men to plough and plant the land. And there were the joyful harvest times when everyone helped to gather the crops, and to crush the grapes and olives. She remembered the happy times talking with her neighbours and friends at the town's well. And each day she had baked fresh bread for her family. Then every evening they ate together, and spoke of all that had happened during that day.

When the two women arrived safely in Bethlehem, the whole town was excited to see them! The women asked if this was really Naomi? But she told them not to call her Naomi, which means "pleasant," but to call her Mara, which means "bitter," because she had left Bethlehem with her family and returned without them. Yet she was not really alone. Ruth had left everything behind to cling to Naomi, her land, her people, and her God.

Ruth

Ruth

The Farming Year In Bethlehem

February — Almond in blossom

January

Main Rains

December Grain Sowing

November

First rains

October Olive Harvest

September Ploughing

Ruth

Barley Harvest

Naomi and Ruth had arrived in Bethlehem at the beginning of the barley harvest. So Ruth asked her mother-in-law if she could gather leftover heads of grain in the field, and Naomi agreed.

Now as Ruth followed the reapers and gathered grain, she ended up in a part of the field that belonged to Boaz. Now Boaz was a respected and wealthy man. And while she was working there, he arrived from Bethlehem. Boaz called to the harvesters, "The LORD be with you!" And they replied, "The LORD bless you!"

When Boaz noticed Ruth, he asked his foreman who the young woman was and where she had come from. And the foreman replied that she had come from Moab with Naomi. After asking his permission to gather grain from among the sheaves, she had been working hard ever since. And she had only had a very short rest.

Ruth

Boaz Meets Ruth

Boaz went over to Ruth and spoke with her. He told her to stay in his field and stay behind the young women. His young men had been warned not to treat her roughly. And when she was thirsty, she could help herself from the water jugs that the young men had filled from the well.

Ruth fell at his feet and thanked him warmly. "What have I done to deserve such kindness?" she asked. "I am only a foreigner."   Ruth 2:10

And Boaz replied that he knew all that she had done for her mother-in-law since the death of her husband. And that she had left her family and her own land to live among strangers. So he spoke a blessing over Ruth.

"May the LORD, the God of Israel, under whose wings you have come to take refuge, reward you fully for what you have done."   Ruth 2:12

When everyone sat down to eat, Boaz called Ruth to join them and share their food. Now Boaz gave Ruth more food than she could eat, so she saved the leftovers for Naomi. When she went back to work, Boaz spoke secretly with his men. He told them to drop barley grain on purpose, so that Ruth could gather it. And he warned them to treat her kindly.

Ruth

Boaz's Goodness to Ruth and Naomi

Ruth gathered barley all that day. Then in the evening, she beat out the grain from the chaff. After all her hard work and Boaz's secret help, she ended up with more than half a bushel of grain! Tired and happy, Ruth carried her sack of grain back to Bethlehem. She showed Naomi what she had gleaned, and also gave her the roasted grain left over from her meal. Well, Naomi was delighted and hoped that God would bless the one who had been kind to her daughter-in-law.

Then Ruth told Naomi that the one she had worked with that day was named Boaz.

"May the LORD bless him!" Naomi told her daughter-in-law. "He is showing his kindness to us as well as to your dead husband. That man is one of our closest relatives, one of our family redeemers." Ruth 2:20

Then Ruth said that Boaz had told her to stay with his workers until the harvest was finished. So Naomi was even more delighted! She would no longer need to worry, because Ruth would be safe in Boaz's field. So Ruth stayed with her mother-in-law, and worked with Boaz's labourers until the end of the barley harvest, and the wheat harvest.

Naomi Advises Ruth

One day, Naomi told Ruth that she must find a good home for her and a suitable husband. Boaz was a close relative of hers, and he had been very kind to Ruth. He would be winnowing barley grain that night. So she advised Ruth to take a bath and put on perfume and wear her nicest clothes. Then go to the threshing floor.

But Naomi warned her to be careful that Boaz didn't see her. After he had finished eating and drinking, she should wait until he had fallen asleep. Then uncover his feet, and lie down. This was an accepted custom in Israel, and would show that Ruth wanted Boaz to be her husband.

Ruth Obeys Her Mother-in-Law

Ruth agreed to do all that her mother-in-law told her, and went down to the threshing floor. After Boaz and his men had finished working, they ate and drank together. Then Boaz laid down at the end of a pile of grain and went to sleep. Ruth then crept quietly from her hiding place, lifted the cover from his feet, and laid down.

Around midnight something startled Boaz, and he woke up to find a woman lying at his feet! He asked who she was.

"I am your servant, Ruth," she replied. "Spread the corner of your covering over me, for you are my family redeemer." Ruth 3:9

Boaz was delighted that Ruth had chosen him and not a younger man, either rich or poor. He told her not to worry about anything, he would do what she had asked. For everyone in Bethlehem knew that she was a good woman.

Boaz Wants To Marry Ruth

Boaz explained that there was a closer relative than himself, and he had the first right to marry Ruth. So in the morning, he would talk to this relative and find out what he wanted to do.

Ruth lay at Boaz's feet all that night. Then she got up before it was light, so no one would know that a woman was at the threshing floor. And Boaz did not want Ruth to return to her mother-in-law empty handed, so he filled her shawl with six measures of barley grain. Then Ruth went home, and Boaz went immediately to the town.

When Naomi asked Ruth what had happened, she told her everything that Boaz had done. And then she gave her mother-in-law the six measures of barley grain. Now Naomi advised Ruth to wait patiently, Boaz would not rest until he had settled the matter that day.

Ruth

Boaz Buys Naomi's Land

Meanwhile, Boaz had gone to the town's gate and sat down there. Now when the relative he had mentioned passed by, Boaz invited him to sit down next to him. Then he called ten leaders from the town to sit with them as witnesses.

Boaz said to the family redeemer, "You know Naomi, who came back from Moab. She is selling the land that belonged to our relative Elimelech. I thought I should speak to you about it so that you can redeem it if you wish. If you want the land, then buy it here in the presence of these witnesses. But if you don't want it, let me know right away, because I am next in line to redeem it after you." The man replied, "All right, I'll redeem it." Ruth 4:3-4

Then Boaz said that his relative's purchase of the land from Naomi also required his marriage to Ruth the Moabite; so that she could have children to carry on her husband's name, and to inherit his land.

After hearing this, the man changed his mind. He didn't want to buy the field and support Naomi and Ruth as well! And he didn't want the field to be inherited by Ruth's future son, instead of members of his own family! So he told Boaz to buy it. Then he took off his sandal and gave it to Boaz as this was the custom to make an agreement legal.

Ruth

Boaz Marries Ruth

Then Boaz told the ten leaders and the people gathered there that they were his witnesses. That day, he was buying the field that belonged to Elimelech and his sons, Kilion and Mahlon, and that he had also chosen to take Ruth the Moabite as his wife.

Then the elders and all the people standing in the gate replied, "We are witnesses! May the LORD make this woman who is coming into your home like Rachel and Leah, from whom all the nation of Israel descended! May you prosper in Ephrathah and be famous in Bethlehem."   Ruth 4:11

Boaz took Ruth to be his wife, and God blessed them with a healthy baby boy. So Ruth was content and at peace. God had richly rewarded her hard work, kindness, and loyalty. He had blessed her with a loving husband, a home, and a son!

* Ephrathah - another name for Bethlehem

Ruth

33

Life Is Pleasant

God had also blessed Naomi. He had brought her back to her land, her friends, and her people. He had also given her a new family. Boaz was her kind protector and provider. While Ruth was better to her than seven sons!

Boaz and Ruth named their son Obed, and Naomi loved her grandson dearly. So Naomi was no longer bitter, lonely, and sad. Her broken heart was healed and she was filled with joy. Life for Naomi was now very pleasant. So when her friends and neighbours saw her nursing Obed, they said, "At last Naomi has a son again!"

Now when Obed became a man and married, he had a son named Jesse. And when Jesse married and had a son, Obed became the grandfather of David, the future king of Israel.

The God of Israel cares for those who are poor.
He comforts those who are brokenhearted.
And He turns their sadness into joy.

Ruth

Ruth

Boaz was the father of Obed

Obed was the father of Jesse

Jesse was the father of King David

RUTH
A young woman loses everything and then finds love.

Study Notes and Questions

When Israel made good choices and decisions, God blessed the nation. But when Israel chose to turn away from Him, there was a famine in the land.

1. Elimelech decided to move his family from Israel to Moab. A land where the people worshipped many idols.
    a. Do you think Elimelech made the right decision?

2. Israelites were not allowed to marry anyone who did not worship the God of Israel.
    a. Who did Mahlon and Kilion marry?

3. Sometimes people blame God for things that happen.
    a. Have you ever done that?
    b. Do you need to ask for His forgiveness?

4. Someone in your life might bring change. You may not like that change.
    a. Do you need to forgive the person?

5. Perhaps Naomi was disappointed when her sons married foreign women.
    a. Did she choose to be kind to her daughters-in-law anyway?

6. Naomi lost her husband and her two sons in Moab.
    a. Did she blame God for this?

7. Naomi decided to return to her own land and her people.
    a. Do you think she made the right decision?

8. Naomi advised her daughters-in-law to return to their parents. Then sets off on her journey alone.
    a. What does Orpah decide to do?
    b. What does Ruth decide to do?
    c. What would you have done?

9. Sometimes we might be afraid of change.
a. Has there been a change in your life?
b. Has that change made you sad, or happy?

.. when I am afraid, I will trust in You. (Psalm 56:3)

10. If we are sad, nothing seems right. Naomi had Ruth's love and support. But when Naomi arrives in Bethlehem she tells friends to call her Mara (which means 'bitter'). Read Isaiah 61:2-7
    a. What are God's promises to those who are sad?

11. Ruth has no husband or children, and she's a stranger in a foreign land. But she is not bitter.
Read Leviticus 19:9-10
    a. How did God provide for the poor and for strangers?

12. Ruth had a good attitude. She worked hard and looked after her mother-in-law. She chose to be patient and kind.

Ruth

Read Exodus 16:1-3

Prayer: Dear Father God, please help me to cope with changes and to always do my best. Forgive me when I'm grumpy and complain. Thank you

13. Ruth respected Naomi. She listened to her advice and obeyed her instructions.
...fools despise wisdom and discipline.   Proverbs 1:7
...those who take advice are wise.   Proverbs 13:10
If you need wisdom, ask our generous God, and He will give it to you. James 1:5

14. Ruth asked if she could glean in the barley field belonging to Boaz.
    a. *Do you think it was God's plan that she should work in his field?*
    b. *When Boaz arrived, what did he say to his workers?*
    c. *When he saw Ruth, what did he do?*
    d. *What had he heard about Ruth?*

15. If one of your fellow Israelites falls into poverty and is forced to sell some family land, then a close relative should buy it back for him. Leviticus 25:25
    a. *Why was Naomi pleased that Ruth was working in Boaz's field?*
    b. *What does she advise Ruth to do?*

16. Ruth obeyed her mother-in-law
    a. *What did Boaz think of Ruth?*
    b. *What did Boaz decide to do right away?*
    c. *What did Naomi advise Ruth to do?*

17. Boaz meets a relative who is more closely related to Naomi
    a. What does Boaz do?
    b. How was his decision made legal?
    c. Who were the witnesses?
    d. How was Ruth rewarded by the God of Israel?

When the people of Israel were slaves in Egypt, God redeemed (rescued) them and led them back to Israel. And all the prophets of Israel wrote about the Messiah, who would come to the Jewish people. He would be their Redeemer (Rescuer).

According to the Jewish law, a redeemer had to be a relative. Jesus was a Jew, a descendant of king David. He was born in Bethlehem and belonged to the tribe (family) of Judah.

God cares about you.

"For I know the plans I have for you," declares the LORD, "plans to heal you and not to harm you, plans to give you a hope and a future." Jeremiah 29:11

Prayer:
Lord Jesus, I want you to be my Redeemer. I believe you died for me. Your blood has paid for my sins and You give me eternal life. Thank You. Amen

Esther

FOREWORD

The Persian Empire spread from India to Ethiopia, and was divided into twenty-seven provinces. The Jewish people, scattered throughout the kingdom, were allowed to keep their own language, customs, and religion.

Esther

Parties at the royal palace

King Xerxes decided to celebrate his third year as ruler of the Persian Empire. He invited all the important people in his kingdom to a party at the royal palace in Susa.

The feast lasted for one hundred and eighty days. During this time, the king showed his guests his many treasures.

Esther

Now the king's humble guests were amazed by the splendour of the gardens. They stared in wonder at the marble pillars, the couches of gold and silver, and the pavements of precious stones. And for seven days, they ate delicious food and drank wine from golden goblets!

Meanwhile, Queen Vashti gave a party for all the women in the royal palace.

Esther

King Xerxes had drunk a lot of wine. On the last day of the feast, he was very happy, and decided to show off his beautiful wife.

So he ordered his servants to bring Queen Vashti to him, wearing her royal crown.

Queen Vashti Insults the King

But when Queen Vashti refused to obey the king's command, he was furious. How dare the queen insult him before all his guests!

The king's anger burned inside him like a fire. He sent for his advisors, those who knew all about the law.

All his advisors agreed together that Queen Vashti had insulted not only the king, but all the people of the Persian Empire! When news of the queen's rebellion spread throughout the kingdom, other women might disobey their husbands too!

Esther

The Search for a New Queen

Queen Vashti was banned from the king's presence forever, and news of her punishment was sent to everyone in the kingdom. Then a search began throughout the king's lands to find a new queen.

Now in the capital city of Susa, there lived a beautiful girl named Hadassah. She was an orphan who had been adopted by her cousin, Mordecai the Jew. But Mordecai had warned Hadassah not to tell anyone that she was Jewish. So she was known by her Persian name, Esther.

Esther and many other lovely girls were chosen and brought to the royal palace. Hegai looked after the girls as they waited to see the king.

For twelve months, each girl received beauty treatments. Now Esther was Hegai's favourite, and he gave her the best rooms in the women's house, special food, and seven servant girls. She had the best of everything!

And everyday, Mordecai walked up and down near the courtyard of the women's quarters to find out how Esther was and what she was doing.

Esther Is Chosen

Eventually, each girl went in before the king. But when Esther's turn came, she pleased him much more than any of the other girls. So the king placed the royal crown on her head and made her queen instead of Vashti.

King Xerxes wanted to show his new queen to all the important people in the kingdom. So he invited them to a special banquet. He declared a holiday for all the people, and gave out many wonderful gifts.

Esther

Mordecai Saves The King's Life

One day, Mordecai was sitting at the king's gate, and he overheard two of the guards at the gate plotting to kill the king!

So Mordecai told Queen Esther what he had heard, and she reported it to the king. Then the two guards were hanged. It was written in the royal journal of events that Mordecai had saved the king's life.

Esther

Haman Plots Against The Jews

Some time later, the king promoted Haman the Agagite to the highest position in his kingdom. All the king's servants had to bow and kneel before Haman. Now the Agagites were enemies of the Jewish people, and Mordecai refused to bow before him!

This puzzled the king's servants. Everyday, they asked Mordecai why he would not obey the king's command. Then at last, Mordecai told them that he was Jewish. So they reported this to Haman.

Haman saw for himself that Mordecai did not bow to him, and he was furious. Then after hearing that Mordecai was a Jew, he vowed to kill not only him, but all the Jews in the Persian kingdom!

Haman's Plot to Kill the Jews

Now the casting of lots was common in ancient times. So at the beginning of the year, in the month of Nissan, the pur - a lot- was thrown before Haman to decide when would be the best time to attack the Jewish people. And it fell on the twelfth month, the month of Adar.

Then Haman went to the king and complained. He said that there was a people in the kingdom with different ways from all the other people, and they did not obey the king's laws. It was not right, and if the king agreed to destroy these people, he would pay for the attack to be carried out.

So the king took off his signet ring and gave it to Haman, the Agagite. He told Haman to go ahead and do whatever he wanted with these people.

Esther

Panic Among the Jews

The king's secretaries wrote out Haman's orders to destroy every Jew on the thirteenth day of the twelfth month. In one day the Jewish people would be wiped out and all their goods taken. The orders were in the king's name and sealed with the king's signet ring. Then royal messengers on horseback delivered the letters to officials throughout the Persian Empire.

As news of the king's terrifying command spread through his lands, there was panic among the Jewish people. They fasted and mourned, and prayed for the God of Israel to help them.

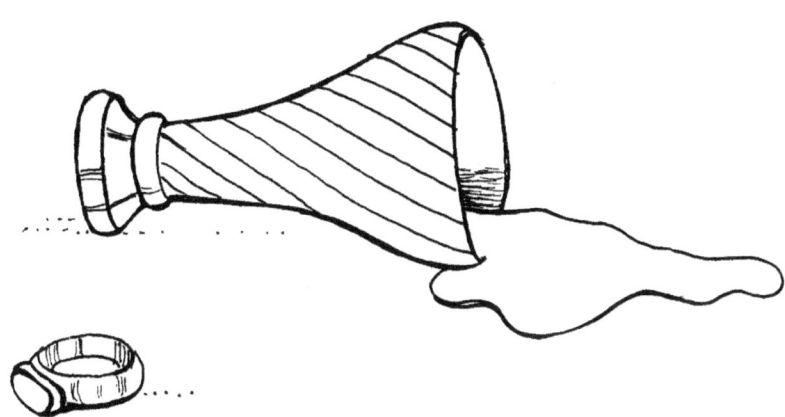

Mordecai Warns Esther

When Mordecai heard the terrible news, he tore his clothes and put on sackcloth and ashes. Then he wandered through the city, weeping for his people.

When Queen Esther's servants told her about Mordecai, she sent him fresh clothes. But he would not accept them. So Esther sent another servant to find out why he was so troubled.

Now the servant met Mordecai outside the king's gate. And after Mordecai had explained all that had happened, he gave the servant a copy of the order to show Esther. He said that she must go to the king and beg him to help them. So the servant hurried back to Queen Esther and reported everything Mordecai had told him.

Esther

Then Esther sent her servant back to Mordecai with this message. Anyone who went before the king without an invitation would be killed, unless the king held out his golden sceptre. And it had been thirty days since she was last invited to see the king.

Of course Mordecai knew all about this law, and he sent Esther a strong warning.

"Don't think for a moment that because you're in the palace you will escape when all other Jews are killed. If you keep quiet at a time like this, deliverance and relief for the Jews will arise from some other place, but you and your relatives will die. Who knows if perhaps you were made queen for such a time as this?" Esther 4:13-14

Queen Esther Risks Her Life

Then Esther sent this reply to Mordecai.

"Go and gather together all the Jews of Susa and fast for me. Do not eat or drink for three days, night or day. My maids and I will do the same. And then, though it is against the law, I will go in to see the king. If I must die, I must die."

So Mordecai went away and did everything as Esther had ordered him.   Esther 4:15-17

Now on the third day of the fast, Queen Esther put on her royal robes and quietly made her way to the inner courtyard. Then she stood opposite the entrance to the king's throne room.

The king was surprised to see Esther standing in the inner courtyard. She looked radiant in her royal garments, and her calm presence pleased the king. So he held out his golden sceptre towards Esther. Then she came near and touched the end of it.

Esther

The king asked her, "What do you want, Queen Esther? What is your request? I will give it to you, even if it is half the kingdom!" Esther 5:3

Esther invited the king and Haman to a banquet that she had prepared. So the king sent for Haman to come quickly. Then they went to Esther's banquet together.

Now while they were drinking wine, the king asked Esther what she wanted. And Esther asked, that if she had pleased the king, would he come with Haman to another banquet the next day? Then she would answer the king's question, and tell him what she wanted.

When Haman left the palace he was a very happy man. Until he saw Mordecai sitting at the palace gate, not getting up, or bowing before him. Then Haman was filled with rage!

Haman's Plan to Kill Mordecai

When he returned home, Haman called together his wife and his friends. Then he boasted about his great riches, his many sons, and his promotion to the highest position in the government.

Then Haman added, "And that's not all! Queen Esther invited only me and the king himself to the banquet she prepared for us. And she has invited me to dine with her and the king again tomorrow!" Then he added, "But this is all worth nothing as long as I see Mordecai the Jew just sitting there at the palace gate." Esther 5:12-13

Then Haman's wife and friends advised him to have a gallows made, seventy feet tall. Then the next morning, he should ask the king's permission to hang Mordecai on it. Haman thought this was an excellent idea! He had the gallows built, and that night he slept very well indeed.

Esther

However, during that same night, the king couldn't sleep. So he ordered his journal of events to be read to him. Now it was written that Mordecai had saved his life, and the king asked if he had been rewarded. His servant replied that nothing had been done.

Mordecai Is Rewarded

The next morning, the king asked his servants if anyone was in the palace courtyard. Well, Haman had just arrived there to ask the king to hang Mordecai. So when his servants said that Haman was waiting, the king told them to bring him in.

Then the king asked Haman what he should do for a man who really pleased him. And proud Haman was very excited. Surely the king was thinking of him!

So he replied, "If the king wishes to honour someone, he should bring out one of the king's own royal robes, as well as a horse that the king himself has ridden on with a royal emblem on its head. Let the robes and the horse be handed over to one of the king's most noble officials. And let him see that the man whom the king wishes to honour is dressed in the king's robes and led through the city square on the king's horse. Have the official shout as they go, 'This is what the king does for someone he wishes to honour!'" Esther 6:7-9

Esther

The king thought this was an excellent idea! He told Haman to go quickly and do everything he had said for Mordecai the Jew, who sat at the palace gate.

So Haman took the robes and put them on Mordecai, the one he hated. Then he placed him on the king's horse, and led him through the city square.

As he went, Haman shouted, "This is what the king does for someone he wishes to honour!" Esther 6:11

Afterwards, Mordecai returned to the palace gate, but Haman hurried home in shame. When his wife and friends heard his news, they gave him a warning. If Mordecai was a Jew, he would not defeat him. Now while they were talking, the king's servants arrived to escort Haman to Queen Esther's banquet.

The King Executes Haman

So the king and Haman went together to eat at Queen Esther's banquet. Again, the king asked Esther what it was that she wanted. And the queen asked him to save her life and the lives of her people. Then she told him of the plot to kill her and her people. The king was shocked and demanded to know who would dare to do such a thing!

Esther replied, "This wicked Haman is our adversary and our enemy." Haman grew pale with fright before the king and queen. Then the king jumped to his feet in a rage and went out into the palace garden. Esther 7:6-7

But Haman remained with Esther and pleaded for his life.

Now when the king returned from the garden, he saw Haman throwing himself on Esther's couch!

The king exclaimed, "Will he even assault the queen right here in the palace, before my very eyes?" And as soon as the king spoke, his attendants covered Haman's face, signalling his doom.   Esther 7:8

Then one of the king's servants told him that Haman had set up gallows in his own courtyard to kill Mordecai the Jew, the man who had saved the king's life.

Filled with rage, the king ordered them to hang Haman on his own gallows! Then the king calmed down.

Mordecai is Honoured

That same day, the king gave Haman's estate to Queen Esther. Now when Esther told him that Mordecai was her relative, the king sent for him. He gave Mordecai his signet ring, and Esther put him in charge of Haman's estate.

Haman's Plot is Defeated

Once again, Esther went before the king. She fell at his feet and begged him to end the evil plans against her people. And the king stretched out his golden sceptre over Esther. So she stood up and asked the king to send out letters to all his provinces, cancelling Haman's order to destroy the Jews. King Xerxes loved Esther and he did all that she requested.

Esther

Immediately, letters were written in the king's name. Then Mordecai sealed them with the king's signet ring. Messengers rode on the king's fastest horses, to deliver the letters to every part of the Persian Empire.

This new order from the king, said that the Jews should join together to defend themselves. And they could kill anyone who tried to attack and rob them.

Now Mordecai left the palace wearing a royal robe and cloak, and with a golden crown on his head. Everyone in Susa had heard about the king's new orders. So Mordecai was greeted with loud and joyful cheers! And in every place where the king's order was delivered, there was feasting and celebrations among the Jewish people.

On the thirteenth day of the twelfth month, the Jews joined together and attacked all those who had planned to destroy them. And every ruler in the Persian Empire helped them because they were afraid of Mordecai. So all the enemies of the Jewish people were killed. And the ten sons of Haman were hanged in the city of Susa.

The Feast of Purim

Mordecai did not want the Jews to forget Haman's wicked plot to destroy them or brave Queen Esther, who God had used to save them from their enemies.

So they were to celebrate every year on the thirteenth and fourteenth of the twelfth month. It would be a special holiday called "Purim," a Persian word for throwing dice, reminding the Jewish people how lots had been thrown to decide the date of their destruction.

Now Mordecai became the most powerful man in the kingdom, except for the king. And everyone lived in peace during his life time.

PRAYER

When we speak to God, He hears and answers.

"I will answer them before they even call to Me. While they are still talking about their needs, I will go ahead and answer their prayers."   Isaiah 65:24

We pray alone.

But when you pray, go away by yourself, shut the door behind you, and pray to your Father in private. Then your Father who sees everything, will reward you."   Matthew 6:6

We pray together.

"Then if My people who are called by My name will humble themselves and pray and seek My face and turn from their wicked ways, I will hear from heaven and will forgive their sins and restore their land."
                              2 Chronicles 7:14

There are times when we fast and pray.

"Go and gather together all the Jews of Susa and fast for me. Do not eat or drink for three days, day or night. My maids and I will do the same. And then, though it is against the law, I will go in to see the king. If I must die, I must die."   Esther 4:16

Esther

A beautiful young orphan becomes the Queen of Persia

Study Notes and Questions

For the LORD Most High is awesome, He is king over all the earth.   Psalm 47:2

On His robe at His thigh was written this title, King of kings and Lord of lords.   Revelation 19:16

The king of Persia's kingdom stretched from Ethiopia to India and he ruled over many peoples.

King Xerxes ruled over the Persian Empire and its many peoples for an allotted time. God is King over all the earth, forever.

Queen Vashti publicly refused to obey King Xerxes. Disrespecting the powerful king was a very foolish and dangerous thing to do. But Vashti didn't give a reason for her behaviour, or an apology.

Pride goes before destruction and haughtiness before a fall.   Proverbs 16:18

What type of person was Queen Vashti?

Esther

Esther won Hegai's favour and he gave her special treatment. Before she visited the king, Esther asked for Hegai's advice and did what he suggested.

Pride leads to conflict; but those who take advice are wise.   Proverbs 13:10

What type of person was Esther?

_____

Esther won the king's favour and she became Queen of Persia

Don't be concerned about the outward beauty of fancy hairstyles, expensive jewellery, or beautiful clothes. You should clothe yourselves instead with the beauty that comes from within, the unfading beauty of a gentle and quiet spirit, which is precious to God.   1 Peter 3:3-4

There were many young and beautiful girls for the king to choose from.

Why do you think he chose Esther?

_____

Esther

Mordecai overheard a plot to kill the king.

What did he do about it?

What do his actions say about his character?

The king promoted Haman the Agagite (Amalekite). But Mordecai refused to bow down to him.

Never forget what the Amalekites did to you (Israel) when you came from Egypt. They attacked you when you were exhausted and weary, and they struck down those who were straggling behind. They had no fear of God.   Deuteronomy 25:17-18

Eglon (king of Moab) enlisted the Ammonites and Amalekites as allies, and he went out and defeated Israel.   Judges 3:13

Why would Mordecai refuse to bow to powerful Haman?

What does this tell us about Mordecai's character?

Esther

Haman plots to kill Mordecai and all the other Jewish people in the Persian Empire.

Don't pick a fight without reason, when no one has done you harm. Proverbs 3:30

> What type of person was Haman?
>
> Why did he want to murder Mordecai and all the Jewish people?

Haman used his position and bribery to win the king's approval for his plan.

"You must never twist justice or show partiality. Never accept a bribe, for bribes blind the eyes of the wise and corrupt the decisions of the godly." Deuteronomy 16:19

> What type of person was King Xerxes?

News of Haman's plot reaches the Jews.

> What is the Jews' reaction?
>
> What does Mordecai ask Queen Esther to do?
>
> What is her first response?

Esther

Mordecai receives Queen Esther's reply.

What message does he send back to Queen Esther?

What was Esther's second response?

———————————————————————

Mordecai, Queen Esther and her maids, and all the Jews in the city of Susa, fasted and prayed for three days.

"Be still in the presence of the LORD, and wait patiently for Him to act. Don't worry about evil people who prosper or fret about their wicked schemes." Psalm 37:7

"My help comes from the LORD, who made heaven and earth." Psalm 121:1

Who did the Jews seek help from?

Who did they trust to give Esther favour with the king?

In times of trouble, what do you do?

"Trust in the LORD with all your heart; do not depend on your own understanding. Seek His will in all you do, and He will show you which path to take." Proverbs 3:5-6

———————————————————————

Esther

After three days Queen Esther went before the king. He gave her permission to come close and asked what she wanted from him. She didn't answer his question, but invited him to a banquet.

A gentle answer deflects anger, but harsh words make tempers flare.   Proverbs 15:1

Commit your actions to the LORD, and your plans will succeed.   Proverbs 16:3

Haman was happy and full of pride when he was invited to dine with the king and queen. However his rage against Mordecai increased. Despite the order to kill all the Jews, Mordecai was still refusing to bow to him!

Even though I walk through the darkest valley, I will not be afraid, for You are close by me.   Psalm 23:4

> *What was Haman's plan against Mordecai?*
>
> *Why wasn't Mordecai afraid of Haman?*
>
> *What fears do you have?*

Esther

One night the king couldn't sleep and he was reminded of Mordecai's action to save his life.

Why did Haman go to see the king the next day?

What did the king ask Hamam?

What was Haman's reply?

Why did Haman suggest this idea to the king?

Who carried out Haman's suggestion?

Pride ends in humiliation, while humility brings honour.
Proverbs 29:23

During difficult times we may lose hope and think there's no justice. But God is not in a hurry. He has a plan. Joseph suffered unjustly for years. But God had a plan for Joseph's life. He would rise to a powerful position in Egypt. Then during a time of famine he would save his family, and many other lives. (Read Genesis 45:4-7.)

And we know that God causes everything to work together for the good of those who love God and are called according to His purposes.... Romans 8:28

Esther

At the second banquet, the king asks Esther what it is that she wants.

> *What does she ask of the king?*
>
> *Why is he shocked at her answer?*

Queen Esther accuses Haman, and he is terrified.

> *How does the king react?*
>
> *What does Haman do?*
>
> *What happens to Haman?*

The king gives Haman's estate to Queen Esther. Then Mordecai is brought before the king and Esther reveals that he is her relative.

The LORD helps them, rescuing them from the wicked. He saves them, and they find shelter in Him.
Psalm 37:40

> *What happens to Haman?*
>
> *What does Queen Esther ask the king to do?*
>
> *What is the king's response?*

105

Esther

Mordecai sent letters in the king's name to all 127 provinces in the king's empire.

> *What rights did the king give to the Jews?*
>
> *How was Mordecai dressed when he left the palace?*
>
> *What did the Jews do when they heard the good news?*

The day arrives when the Jews' enemies planned to kill them. But the opposite happens, the Jews destroy their tormentors!
On that day the king asks Queen Esther what more she wanted. If she told him, he would do it.

> *What did Queen Esther ask?*
>
> *What happened in the city of Susa?*

Mordecai sent letters to all the Jews instructing them to celebrate this victory every year.

You have turned my mourning into joyful dancing. You have taken away my clothes of mourning and clothed me with joy.   Psalm 30:11

> *What did God do for all the Jews in the Persian Empire?*
>
> *How did the Jews celebrate?*

Esther

What was the name of this annual celebration?

_____

Mordecai the Jew became the prime minister, with authority next to that of King Xerxes himself. Esther 10:3

The wise inherit honour, but fools He holds to shame. Proverbs 3:35

_____

Prayer

"If My people who are called by My name will humble themselves and pray and seek My face and turn from their wicked ways, I will hear from heaven and will forgive their sins and restore their land." 2 Chronicles 7:14

LORD, you know the hopes of the helpless. Surely you will hear their cries and comfort them. Psalm 10:17

You answer our prayers. All of us must come to You. Though we are overwhelmed by our sins, you forgive them all. Psalm 65:2-3

Moses and Aaron were among His priests; Samuel also called on His name. They cried to Him for help, and He answered them. Psalm 99:6

Thanking God

David's Song of Praise

Give thanks to the LORD
and proclaim His greatness.
Let the whole world know what He has done.
Sing to Him; yes, sing His praises.
Tell everyone about His wonderful deeds.
1 Chronicles 16:8-9

A Psalm of David

Praise the LORD!
For He has heard my cry for mercy.
The LORD is my strength and shield.
I trust in Him with all my heart.
He helps me, and my heart is filled with joy.
I burst into songs of thanksgiving.
Psalm 28:6-7

Thanksgiving

Enter His gates with thanksgiving;
enter His courts with praise.
Give thanks to Him and praise His name.
Psalm 100:4

Prayer and Fasting

In times of urgent prayer to God, His people did not eat or drink. Other customs in times of distress and mourning were tearing clothing, dressing in sackcloth, and throwing dust and ashes on the head. But God made it clear that a change of heart was what was really needed.

Job's Prayer to the LORD

You asked, "Who is this that questions My wisdom with such ignorance?' "It is I and I was talking about things I knew nothing about. Job 42:2

I take back everything I said, and I sit in dust and ashes to show my repentance." Job 42:6

A Call to Repentance

Don't tear your clothing in your grief, but tear your hearts instead. Return to the LORD your God, for He is merciful and compassionate. Joel 2:13

PURIM
The Feast of Esther

The Jewish people still celebrate Purim on the fourteenth and fifteenth of Adar, the twelfth month of the biblical year.

When the Book of Esther is read in the synagogues, Mordecai's name is greeted with happy cheers. But at the name of Haman, there are shouts of disapproval, everyone stamps their feet and make a lot of noise with rattles and shakers!

Purim is a joyful time. The children have painted faces, and some wear masks and colourful costumes. Gifts of food are sent to friends and to the poor. There are delicious traditional pastries to eat and in the late afternoon a celebration meal is enjoyed.

The laws and customs of Purim all stem from the Book of Esther. This wonderful story of good triumphing over evil reminds everyone that the unseen God is in control and He acts to save His people.

Mordecai and Esther loved God and lived by His laws. When they prayed for God's help, He rescued His people from being slaughtered. He also honoured and rewarded Mordecai and Esther. Everyone was relieved and delighted at what God had done, so they celebrated.

What God did for His people was recorded in the Bible. And so they would not forget, God told them to celebrate this event every year.

If you too would like to belong to God, you could say this simple prayer.

Thank You Jesus that You died for my sins, so that I can be forgiven and live free from guilt. I want to know and love You. And I believe that You will answer my prayer. Amen

Name:

Date:

Esther

Esther

About the Author

God gave British author Pauline Shone a very special gift. It was the gift of creativity. And at seven years old, she made her first illustration, Prince Charming dancing with Cinderella! And at sixteen years of age, she began a five years Art College Degree Course. This led to a career in teaching, and then as a designer and sculptor for the ceramic industry. But after coming to a personal faith in Jesus as her Saviour, she used her God-given gift for Him. Over many years she created a series of illustrated Bible Stories for children.

Books by the Author

Feed My Lambs series, colouring books:

Feed My Sheep series,
Bible story colouring books:

 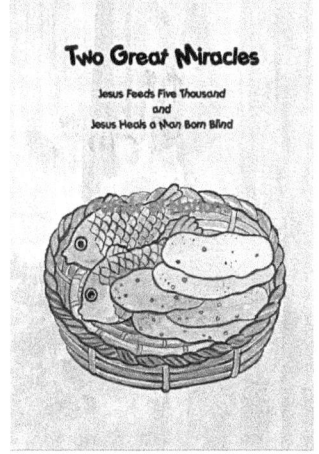 

Bible story books

Bible study book for teens

Bible story picture book full colour, hard cover:

Adult paperback books:

www.ingramcontent.com/pod-product-compliance
Lightning Source LLC
Chambersburg PA
CBHW040553010526
44110CB00054B/2673